CREATIVE WRITING PROMP
AGES 8-12

this Book Belongs to:

Table of Contents
Story Prompts

Welcome to Your Writing Adventure!

Hello, Young Writer!
Are you ready to start on an incredible journey where your imagination is the map and your pen is the compass? If you're eager to dive into worlds filled with mysteries, magic, and more, then you've picked up the right book!

This book is your ticket to adventure, packed with 55 fun story prompts that will whisk you away from your everyday life. From talking animals and magical forests to time-traveling escapades and mysterious, far-off planets, every page offers a new doorway to adventure.

But that's not all! Each prompt comes with questions designed to help you dive deeper into your stories. These questions will challenge you to think creatively, solve problems, and explore your characters and plots in exciting ways. They're your trusty tools to build and navigate through your tales.

Whether you're weaving a story about a secret garden that blooms in the heart of a bustling city, or about a lost underwater city guarded by mermaids, this book is here to guide you. You can write about what you imagine, change the endings to your liking, and create characters that have never been dreamt of before.

Remember, there are no limits in the world of creative writing. The wilder your ideas, the better! So grab your pen, open this book to any page, and see where your imagination takes you.

Adventure awaits, and the stories you'll tell are as unlimited as the stars in the night sky. Let's get started and unleash the power of your creativity!

Happy Writing!

Quick Tips for Your Creative Writing Adventure!

- <u>Set Up Your Space</u>: Choose a quiet, cozy spot where you can write without interruptions.

- <u>Gather Your Tools</u>: Keep your favorite writing tools—like pens, pencils or markers ready at your creative spot.

- <u>Read the Prompts Carefully</u>: Think about the prompt deeply and visualize or imagine where it can take you. What's the first image or idea that pops into your head? Start there!

- <u>Use the Questions</u>: Use the questions provided to add depth to your story and explore new ideas. Answer the questions in your head or write down ideas as the bubble up.

- <u>Let Your Imagination Run Wild</u>: There are no wrong answers in creative writing, so think big and be unique!

- <u>Write Regularly</u>: Write a bit every day to improve your skills, just like practicing a sport. The more you write, the better you'll get at it.

- <u>Don't Worry About Mistakes</u>: Spelling errors? Messy handwriting? Weird story ideas? No problem! Focus on getting your ideas down first; you can always edit later.

- <u>Share Your Stories</u>: When you're ready, show your stories to someone you trust, like a family member, a friend, or a teacher. They can offer encouragement, help you improve, and even give you new ideas!

- <u>Make Space for Brainstorming</u>: Use the extra "Story Idea" pages at the end of the book for your story ideas. Record any random ideas that come to you; they might turn into a story later -- maybe your best one yet!

- <u>HAVE FUN!</u> Enjoy the process of writing. If it stops being fun, take a break and return when you're inspired. Remember, every story you write is a reflection of <u>YOUR</u> awesome imagination!

1: A Magical Key

You wake up one morning to find a magical key on your bedside table. this key can open any door, but only once. You decide to use it to open a mysterious door you've never noticed before in your school. What happens when you turn the key and step through the door?

What kind of world or place do you discover on the other side of the door?

3

How do you find your way back home?

Who do you meet in this new place, and how do they help you on your adventure?

2: A Dusty Old Book

While exploring the attic of your grandparent's old house, you stumble upon an ancient, dusty book. As you open it, you're transported to a medieval kingdom where dragons, unicorns, knights, and wizards exist. You are now the hero of this kingdom. What mission are you given, and how do you start your adventure?

What kind of dragon, or wizard do you meet first, and what advice do they give you?

What is the biggest obstacle you encounter during your mission, and how do you solve it?

How does your adventure in the medieval kingdom change you, and what do you bring back with you when you return to the attic?

3: A Hidden Treasure Map

You find an old treasure map hidden inside a library book. the map leads to a secret location in your town. You decide to follow the map's clues with your best friend. What do you discover at the end of your journey?

What are some of the clues on the map, and how do you solve them?

What obstacles do you encounter along the way, and how do you overcome them?

What is the treasure you find, and how does it change your life?

4: A Mysterious Letter

One day, you receive a letter from a mysterious school of magic inviting you to attend. When you arrive, you realize you have a special power that no one else has. What is your unique power, and how do you use it to help your new friends at the school?

How do you first discover your unique power, and how do you feel about it?

What challenges do you face in learning to control your power, and who helps you along the way?

How do you use your power to solve a big problem at the school?

5: A Little Dragon

You wake up to find a small dragon curled up at the foot of your bed. It seems friendly and seems to understand your language. today, you decide to take the dragon to school with you. What happens next?

How do you hide the dragon from your teachers and classmates, and what fun or trouble does it cause during the day?

How does the day end with your new dragon friend, and what do you plan to do next with it?

6: A Book Traveler

You invent a machine that allows you to travel into your favorite book. You decide to test it out and find yourself in the middle of the story. What book do you choose, and what part do you play in the story?

How do the characters from the book react to your arrival, and what role do you take on in the story?

What changes do you make to the plot, and how do they affect the outcome?

How do you manage to return to the real world, and what do you bring back with you?

7: A tiny Alien Spaceship

One evening, a shooting star lands in your backyard, and you find a tiny alien spaceship. the aliens inside ask for your help to repair their ship so they can return home. How do you help them, and what adventures do you go on together?

What are the aliens like, and what do you learn about their home planet?

What tools or materials do you need to fix the spaceship, and where do you find them?

What challenges do you face while repairing the ship, and how do you overcome them?

8: Pen Pals in Space

You receive a letter from a pen pal who lives on another planet. What does the letter say, and how do you reply?

What unique things do you learn about life on another planet from your pen pal?

What do you ? How do you share your own world with your alien friend in your reply?

9: A Hidden Attic Door

While cleaning out your attic, you discover a hidden door that leads to a parallel universe where everything is the opposite of what you know. How do you navigate this strange new world, and what adventure do you have there?

What are some of the biggest differences between your world and the parallel universe, and how do you adapt to them?

Who do you meet in the parallel universe that becomes your ally or enemy?

10: All About the Weather

You receive a mysterious package in the mail with no return address. Inside, you find a strange device that can control the weather. What do you do with this device, and what unexpected events unfold because of your actions?

How do you first test the device, and what weather changes do you make?

What are the consequences of altering the weather, both positive and negative?

_____

_____

_____

_____

_____

_____

_____

_____

_____

_____

_____

_____

_____

_____

11: A Mysterious Hidden Island

You and your family go on a vacation aboard a luxurious cruise ship. One night, the ship encounters a powerful storm and is transported to a mysterious, hidden island. What strange and magical things do you discover on the island?

Who do you meet on the island, and what role do they play in your adventure?

What unique plants and animals do you find on the island, and how do they help or hinder you?

12: the Sunken Pirate Ship

While snorkeling near a coral reef, you find a hidden underwater cave. Inside, you discover a sunken pirate ship filled with treasure. What challenges do you face as you explore the pirate ship, and what secrets do you uncover?

What types of sea creatures do you encounter near the coral reef and inside the cave?

What is the most valuable or interesting piece of treasure you find, and what do you do with it?

_____

_____

_____

_____

_____

_____

_____

_____

_____

_____

13: Dolphins in Distress

You are part of a team of marine biologists on a research vessel. One day, you receive a distress signal from a group of dolphins that leads you to an underwater city inhabited by mermaids. How do you help the mermaids, and what adventures do you have in their underwater city?

How do the mermaids thank you for your help, and what do you learn from this experience?

What incredible sights and creatures do you encounter in the underwater city?

_____

_____

_____

_____

_____

_____

_____

_____

_____

14: Ghost Ship

During a sailing trip with your friends, you come across an abandoned ghost ship drifting in the middle of the ocean. As you explore the ship, you realize it holds clues to a long-lost treasure. What happens as you try to uncover the mystery of the ghost ship?

What clues do you find that lead you to the treasure, and where do they take you?

How do you and your friends work together to solve the mystery and find the treasure?

15: A Magical Seashell

You discover a magical seashell on the beach that allows you to talk to sea creatures. With the help of your new underwater friends, you embark on a mission to stop an environmental disaster threatening the ocean. What do you do to save the ocean and its inhabitants?

What types of sea creatures do you befriend, and how do they assist you in your mission?

What environmental disaster is threatening the ocean, and what causes it?

16: the Hidden Cave

During a camping trip, you and your friends discover a hidden cave with glowing crystals. As you explore the cave, you find that the crystals have magical properties. What happens when you touch one of the crystals, and how does it change your adventure?

What magical properties do the crystals have, and how do they affect you and your friends?

What dangers do you encounter inside the cave, and how do you escape them?

What do you learn from this adventure, and how does it affect your future camping trips?

17: A talking Parrot

On the way home from school, you discover a talking parrot that claims to know the way to a hidden pirate treasure. Curious, you decide to follow its directions. What do you discover on this unexpected treasure hunt?

What challenges do you face on the way to finding the treasure, and how do you overcome them?

What do you discover about yourself and your true desires during this journey?

18: A Magic Compass

You receive a mysterious package with a magic compass inside. the compass doesn't point north; instead, it points to whatever you most desire. One Saturday, you decide to follow it. Where does it lead you, and what do you find?

What surprising places does the magic compass take you to, and who do you meet along the way?

What do you discover about yourself and your true desires during this journey?

_____

_____

_____

_____

_____

_____

_____

_____

_____

_____

19: talking Plants

During a hike through the local forest, you stumble upon a hidden, enchanted garden where all the plants can talk. the plants urgently ask for your help. What problem are they facing, and how do you help them solve it?

What unique solutions do you come up with to assist the talking plants?

How does helping the garden affect its future and your relationship with nature?

20: A New Invention

You invent a new smartphone app that can translate animal thoughts into human language. To test it out, you visit the local zoo. What surprising things do you learn from the animals, and how does it affect your visit?

What is the most surprising or profound thing an animal tells you, and how do you respond?

How does this new understanding of animals change your actions or thoughts about them?

_____

_____

_____

_____

_____

_____

_____

_____

_____

21: New Sneakers

You find a pair of sneakers at a garage sale that can make you run faster than a car. The first time you try them out, you accidentally end up miles away from home. Where do you end up, and what adventures do you have along the way?

What interesting places or unexpected challenges do you encounter during your high-speed adventure?

How do you find your way back home, and who helps you along the way?

22: Tiny Aliens

In your backyard, you discover tiny alien robots hiding behind a bush. they're friendly and seems to be looking for something important on Earth. How do you help them, and what do they teach you in return?

What are the robots searching for, and how do you assist in their mission?

What important lessons about technology or the universe do you learn from your new robotic friends?

23: Ancient Egypt

During a family trip to a museum, you touch a mysterious artifact and are transported back in time to ancient Egypt. You must find a way back to the present, but first, you're mistaken for a royal. What happens in ancient Egypt, and how do you convince someone to help you return?

What roles or duties are you expected to perform as a mistaken royal, and how do you handle them?

Who do you befriend in the past, and how do they help you find your way back to your time?

24: Underground Clubhouse

While exploring a new park, you and your friends discover a secret underground clubhouse. Inside, there's a map to a hidden urban treasure. What steps do you take to find it, and what obstacles do you encounter along the way?

What clever tricks or tools do you use to solve the clues on the map?

What is the treasure, and how does finding it impact your friendship and your neighborhood?

25: the Blank Book

You receive a mysterious blank book for your birthday. the next morning, whatever you draw or write in the book becomes real. What is the first thing you create, and how does it change your day?

What challenges do you face with your new creations, and how do you solve them?

How do you decide what to create next, and what rules do you set for yourself?

26: A Fantastical World

Every night, your dreams transport you to a fantastical world where you are a knight tasked with protecting a magical kingdom. One morning, you realize the kingdom is real when a creature from your dreams appears at your door. What happens next?

How do you keep the magical creature safe in the real world, and what dangers follow it from the dream world?

What mission must you complete to ensure the safety of both the dream and real worlds?

27: Mayor for the Day!

You win a contest that allows you to be the mayor of your town for a day. With great power comes great responsibility—and fun! What changes do you implement, and how do the townspeople react?

What is the most surprising or challenging part of being mayor for a day?

How do your decisions as mayor affect your school and neighborhood?

_____

_____

_____

_____

_____

_____

_____

_____

_____

28: An ancient Scroll

While digging in your garden, you unearth an ancient scroll that reveals the location of a hidden mystical grove in your town. What do you discover in the grove, and who else is interested in its secrets?

What magical or unusual plants and creatures do you find in the grove?

How do you protect the grove's secrets from those who might misuse them?

29: A Virtual Reality Game

A new virtual reality game allows you to enter any book or movie as a character. Which story do you choose to enter first, and what role do you play?

How does your presence change the story, and what new adventures do you experience?

What lessons do you learn from living inside a story, and how do you apply them when you return to the real world?

30: A Magical Bracelet

You find a bracelet that allows you to understand and speak any language. What is the first conversation you have, and with whom?

What do you learn from this experience of speaking different languages?

How do you use your new ability to help someone in need?

_____

_____

_____

_____

_____

_____

_____

_____

_____

_____

31: the Mysterious Fog

A mysterious fog rolls into town, and with it comes creatures from folklore. You team up with your friends to uncover the source of the fog and find a way to send the creatures back. What strategies do you use, and what allies do you gain?

What folklore creatures do you encounter, and how do you communicate with them?

What is the source of the fog, and how do you successfully restore order to your town?

32: the Magic Feather

A mysterious rainbow-colored bird visits your window every morning. One day, it drops a shimmering feather that grants you the power to understand and speak to animals. What do you do first with this new ability?

What do you learn from talking to the animals in your neighborhood?

How do you use your new skills to solve a problem an animal friend is facing?

33: Old Goggles

You discover a pair of old goggles that allow you to see through walls. On your way to school, you notice something unusual in an abandoned house. What do you see and what do you decide to do about it?

How do you investigate the mysterious sight without getting into trouble?

What surprising discoveries do you make inside the abandoned house?

_____

_____

_____

_____

_____

_____

_____

_____

_____

_____

34: the Science Experiment

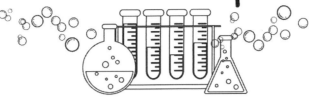

During a science fair, your experiment unexpectedly opens a portal to another dimension. A friendly creature emerges and asks for your help. What is the creature's problem, and how do you help it?

What challenges do you face in trying to help the creature return to its dimension?

What do you learn about the universe and other dimensions from this experience?

_____

_____

_____

_____

_____

_____

_____

_____

_____

_____

_____

35: An Enchanted Atlas

You receive an enchanted atlas for your birthday that lets you teleport to any place you point to on its pages. Which place do you visit first, and what adventures await you there?

What unexpected situations do you find yourself in during your travels?

How does this new ability change your perspective on the world?

_____

_____

_____

_____

_____

_____

_____

_____

_____

36: Superpowered Ice Cream

A new ice cream shop in town serves magical ice cream that gives temporary superpowers. What flavor do you choose, and what power does it give you?

What do you do with your superpower while it lasts?

How do you help someone with the power you received from the ice cream?

37: Dear Diary

You find a diary in your attic that predicts future events. It has an entry about something that will happen tomorrow. What does the diary predict, and how do you prepare for it?

How do you feel as the predicted event approaches, and how do you handle the outcome?

What do you decide to do with the diary afterward?

38: A Secret Mission

Your pet dog starts speaking in perfect English one morning, revealing a secret mission. What is the mission, and how do you get involved?

What challenges do you face while helping your dog with its mission?

How does your relationship with your pet change after sharing this adventure?

39: A Solar Eclipse

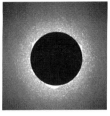

A sudden solar eclipse reveals hidden messages in the sky, visible only during the event. What do the messages say, and what quest do they set you on?

Who do you choose to share this quest with, and why?

What obstacles do you encounter while trying to decode the sky messages further?

40: Robot

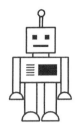

You win a competition and the prize is a day spent with a robot that can do anything. What do you ask the robot to do, and how does it turn out?

What unexpected problems arise from the robot's actions, and how do you solve them?

How does spending the day with the robot change your thoughts on technology and its capabilities?

41: the Stopwatch

You discover a mysterious stopwatch that can freeze time when you press it. the first time you use it, you explore your town as everything else stands still. What do you discover during this frozen time?

What do you choose to do while everyone else is frozen, and why?

How does this experience change your view of the people and places around you?

_____

_____

_____

_____

_____

_____

_____

_____

_____

42: the Stone & the trees

Please help us

Hi

While playing in the forest, you find a mystical stone that allows you to talk with trees. the trees tell you about a coming danger threatening the forest. How do you help them?

What kind of danger is the forest facing, and how do you plan to stop it?

What do you learn from the trees about nature and how to protect it?

43: the Changing Weather

You invent a device that can change the local weather. On its first trial, you create a snow day in the middle of summer. What unexpected consequences does your weather experiment have?

How does the community react to your sudden snow day?

What problems arise from this unusual weather, and how do you fix them?

44: the Mysterious Map

At a local fair, you win a mysterious map in a raffle. It claims to lead to a hidden realm within your city. Curious, you follow the map. What do you find at the end of the trail?

Who or what guides you on your journey to the hidden realm?

What challenges do you encounter in this new place, and how do you overcome them?

45: the Writing Book

You find a book in the library that writes its own story based on the reader's thoughts. When you start reading, you find yourself as the main character. What story unfolds?

How does the story change as your thoughts and emotions change?

What lesson does the book teach you by the end of the story?

_____

_____

_____

_____

_____

_____

_____

_____

_____

_____

46: the Magical Pencil

You receive a magical pencil that brings drawings to life. One afternoon, you draw a creature from your imagination. Surprisingly, it jumps off the page! What is the creature like, and what adventures do you have together?

What is the first thing your new creature friend wants to do in the real world?

How do you handle the challenges of having a magical creature in your life?

47: the Mysterious Maze

A new park opens in your town with a maze that changes its paths every night. You and your friends decide to solve the maze, but you discover it's not an ordinary maze. What makes it unique, and what do you find at its center?

What are the unusual features of the maze, and how do they challenge you?

What is hidden at the center of the maze, and how does it affect your life?

48: the Puppy and the Map

You find a lost puppy in your neighborhood with a collar that has a map attached instead of a name tag. You decide to follow the map. Where does it lead you?

What interesting places or items do you find along the way while following the map?

Who joins you on this adventure, and how do they help you and the puppy?

49: the Parrot and the Lost Friend

During a school trip to the zoo, one of the parrots starts talking to you, asking for help to find its lost friend. How do you help the parrot?

What clues do you and the parrot use to find its friend at the zoo?

How does helping the parrot change your view of animals and friendships?

50: the Flying Skateboard

Your new skateboard can fly! Where do you go on your first flight, and what do you see from the sky?

Your new skateboard can fly! Where do you go on your first flight, and what do you see from the sky?

Who do you show your flying skateboard to, and what is their reaction?

51: the Unusual Seeds

A mysterious bird keeps dropping unusual seeds in your backyard. You decide to plant one. What grows from it?

What special characteristics does the plant have, and how do you care for it?

How does this mysterious plant affect your family or neighbors?

52: My Hamster, the Builder

 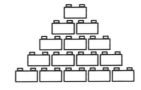

Your pet hamster starts building enormous structures at night. What does it build, and why?

How do you react to your hamster's unexpected skills, and what do you do to support its building projects?

What do you discover about your hamster's creations that surprises you?

53: A Magical Amulet & a Dinosaur

You find an ancient amulet buried in your backyard. When you put it on, you are transported to a time long ago when dinosaurs roamed the Earth. You must find a way to return home while avoiding the dangers of this prehistoric world. What happens during your adventure?

What kind of dragon, what types of dinosaurs do you encounter, and how do you interact with them?

What is the biggest challenge you face, and how do you solve it to make your way back to the present?

54: Mirror, Mirror on the Wall

The Future

Your mirror starts acting as a portal on weekends. Where does it take you this Saturday?

What challenges do you face in the new world you visit through the mirror?

Who do you meet there, and how do they help you navigate their world?

55: A Recycle Gadget

A local inventor gives you a gadget that can recycle anything into something new. What is the first thing you recycle, and what do you make from it?

How does your new invention change the way you and others view recycling?

What creative projects do you do with this gadget, and what impact do they have on your community?

Brainstorming Zone:
For all your Story Sparks!

thank You!

 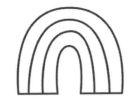 

thank you so much for purchasing our **Creative Writing Prompts for Kids.** We truly appreciate your support and hope that your child/young person loves creating magical stories!

Please Scan the QR Code below to leave us a review; your feedback helps us continue to create engaging and educational books for children and adults.

Find my author page here. Check out all our other great books for kids and adults.

amazon.com/author/littleworldpress

Made in the USA
Columbia, SC
21 October 2024

44846176R00070